GIFTED & TALENTED®

*To develop
your child's gifts
and talents*

MATH
BOOK TWO

A Workbook for Ages 6–8

Written by Martha Cheney
Illustrated by Larry Nolte

D1364025

LOWELL HOUSE JUVENILE

LOS ANGELES

NTC/Contemporary Publishing Group

Published by Lowell House
A division of NTC/Contemporary Publishing Group, Inc.
4255 West Touhy Avenue, Lincolnwood (Chicago), Illinois 60646-1975 U.S.A.

Managing Director and Publisher: Jack Artenstein
Director of Publishing Services: Rena Copperman
Editorial Director, Juvenile: Brenda Pope-Ostrow
Director of Art Production: Bret Perry
Educational Editor: Linda Gorman
Typesetter: Carolyn Wendt

Lowell House books can be purchased at special discounts when ordered in bulk
for premiums and special sales. Please contact Customer Service at:
NTC/Contemporary Publishing Group
4255 W. Touhy Avenue
Lincolnwood, IL 60646-1975
1-800-323-4900

Printed and bound in the United States of America

ISBN: 1-56565-666-0

10 9 8 7 6 5 4 3 2

GIFTED & TALENTED® WORKBOOKS will help develop your child's natural talents and gifts by providing activities to enhance critical and creative thinking skills. These skills of logic and reasoning teach children **how to think**. They are precisely the skills emphasized by teachers of gifted and talented children.

Thinking skills are the skills needed to be able to learn anything at any time. Unlike events, words, and teaching methods, thinking skills never change. If a child has a grasp of how to think, school success and even success in life will become more assured. In addition, the child will become self-confident as he or she approaches new tasks with the ability to think them through and discover solutions.

GIFTED & TALENTED® WORKBOOKS present these skills in a unique way, combining the basic subject areas of reading, language arts, and math with thinking skills. The top of each page is labeled to indicate the specific thinking skill developed. Here are some of the skills you will find:

- Deduction—the ability to reach a logical conclusion by interpreting clues

- Understanding Relationships—the ability to recognize how objects, shapes, and words are similar or dissimilar; to classify or categorize

- Sequencing—the ability to organize events, numbers; to recognize patterns

- Inference—the ability to reach a logical conclusion from given or assumed evidence

- Creative Thinking—the ability to generate unique ideas; to compare and contrast the same elements in different situations; to present imaginative solutions to problems

How to Use GIFTED & TALENTED® WORKBOOKS

Each book contains activities that challenge children. The activities range from easier to more difficult. You may need to work with your child on many of the pages, especially with the child who is a non-reader. However, even a non-reader can master thinking skills, and the sooner your child learns how to think, the better. Read the directions to your child and, if necessary, explain them. Let your child choose to do the activities that interest him or her. When interest wanes, stop. A page or two at a time may be enough, as the child should have fun while learning.

It is important to remember that these activities are designed to teach your child **how to think**, not how to find the right answer. Teachers of gifted children are never surprised when a child discovers a new "right" answer. For example, a child may be asked to choose the object that doesn't belong in this group: a table, a chair, a book, a desk. The best answer is **book**, since all the others are furniture. But a child could respond that all of them belong because they all could be found in an office or a library. The best way to react to this type of response is to praise the child and gently point out that there is another answer, too. While creativity should be encouraged, your child must look for the best and most **suitable** answer.

GIFTED & TALENTED® WORKBOOKS have been written and endorsed by educators. These books will benefit any child who demonstrates curiosity, imagination, a sense of fun and wonder about the world, and a desire to learn. They will open your child's mind to new experiences and help fulfill his or her true potential.

Addition Patterns

Solve the addition problems below. Look for the pattern created by the answers.

1	2	3	4	5
+ 0	+ 1	+ 2	+ 3	+ 4

6	7	8	9
+ 5	+ 6	+ 7	+ 8

If there were one more problem, what do you think its answer would be? _____

Color in the squares below that have the answers to the problems and question above.

10	7	15	1
8	11	4	9
12	19	3	17
20	16	14	13
6	2	18	5

What pattern do the colored squares make? _____

More Addition Patterns

Solve the addition problems below. Look for the pattern created by the answers.

$$\begin{array}{r} 4 \\ +\ 2 \\ \hline \end{array} \qquad \begin{array}{r} 1 \\ +\ 6 \\ \hline \end{array} \qquad \begin{array}{r} 5 \\ +\ 3 \\ \hline \end{array} \qquad \begin{array}{r} 7 \\ +\ 2 \\ \hline \end{array}$$

$$\begin{array}{r} 5 \\ +\ 5 \\ \hline \end{array} \qquad \begin{array}{r} 3 \\ +\ 8 \\ \hline \end{array} \qquad \begin{array}{r} 10 \\ +\ 2 \\ \hline \end{array} \qquad \begin{array}{r} 9 \\ +\ 4 \\ \hline \end{array}$$

Create two new problems that continue the pattern of answers.

$$+\ \underline{\qquad} \qquad +\ \underline{\qquad}$$

Color in the squares below that have the answers to the problems above.

14	8	11
3	16	6
5	15	13
17	4	9
7	10	12

What pattern do the colored squares make? _____

Add and Spell

Solve each of the addition problems below.

W	P	A	S	O	I
3	4	5	9	8	9
4	4	5	4	3	7
+ 2	+ 4	+ 5	+ 1	+ 5	+ 3

T	B	L	V	Y	E
7	6	4	3	1	7
2	6	6	7	1	7
+ 4	+ 6	+ 7	+ 0	+ 6	+ 7

Now write the letter that corresponds to each answer on the line where the answer appears. You will spell out some good advice!

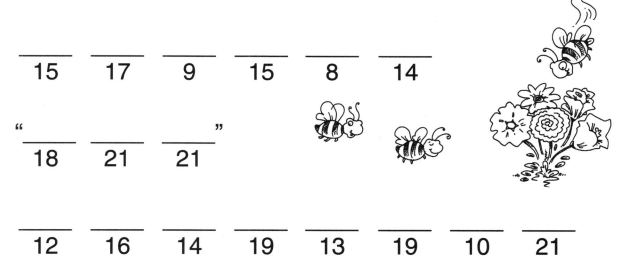

$\overline{}$ $\overline{}$ $\overline{}$ $\overline{}$ $\overline{}$ $\overline{}$
15   17   9   15   8   14

"$\overline{}$ $\overline{}$ $\overline{}$"
18   21   21

$\overline{}$ $\overline{}$ $\overline{}$ $\overline{}$ $\overline{}$ $\overline{}$ $\overline{}$ $\overline{}$
12   16   14   19   13   19   10   21

Do you think this advice is easy to follow? Why or why not?

Mystery Numbers

Fill in the missing numbers in each addition series.

1 + ___ = 2 + ___ = 5 + 3 = ___

4 + ___ = ___ + 2 = 7 + ___ = 9

2 + 2 = ___ + ___ = 7 + ___ = 10

___ + 3 = ___ + 2 = 8 + ___ = 12

___ + 4 = ___ + 3 = ___ + 2 = 15

6 + ___ = ___ + 2 = 14 + ___ = 18

Number Bull's-Eye

Fill in each empty space on the dartboard with a number. Each number must make each addition problem add up to the sum shown in the center.

One problem has been done for you.

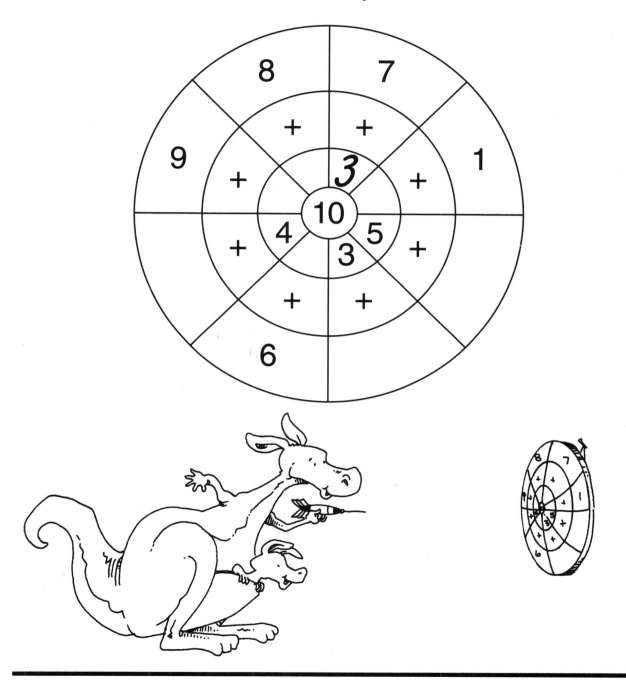

ABC Addition

Each letter of the alphabet has been given a number value.

A	B	C	D	E	F	G	H	I	J	K	L	M
1	2	3	4	5	6	7	8	9	10	11	12	13

Add the value of the letters for each boxed word on this page and the next. One word has been done for you.

HAT

H = 8
A = 1
T = 20

8 + 1 + 20 = 29

PIG

BOX

MAN

N	O	P	Q	R	S	T	U	V	W	X	Y	Z
14	15	16	17	18	19	20	21	22	23	24	25	26

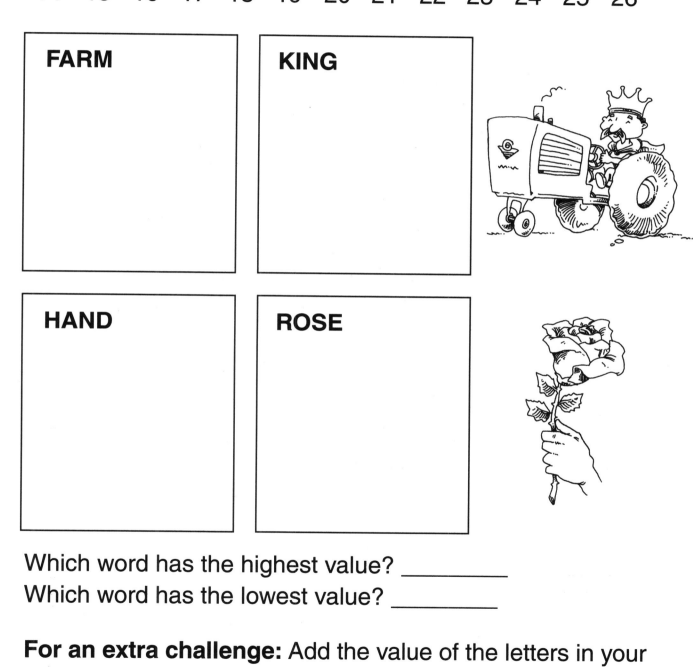

FARM

KING

HAND

ROSE

Which word has the highest value? _____

Which word has the lowest value? _____

For an extra challenge: Add the value of the letters in your name. What is the sum? _____

Across the Ice

Penny the Penguin is playing a game with her friends. She must find a path across the icebergs that adds up to 18. She may only swim between icebergs that are joined by lines.

Draw a path through the icebergs to show Penny the way.

Hint: There may be more than one path!

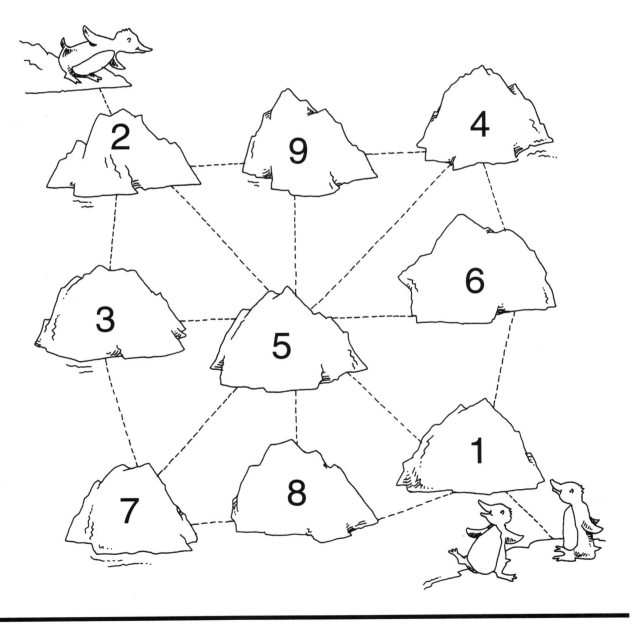

Number Bull's-Eye

Fill in each empty space on the dartboard with a number. Each number must make each addition problem add up to the sum shown in the center.

One problem has been done for you.

Through the Forest

Eddie the Elf has found some interesting toadstools growing in the forest. Each toadstool has a number on it! Eddie has made up a game to play on his way home. He wants to find the path through the toadstools that has the lowest sum.

Draw a line through the toadstools to show Eddie the way.

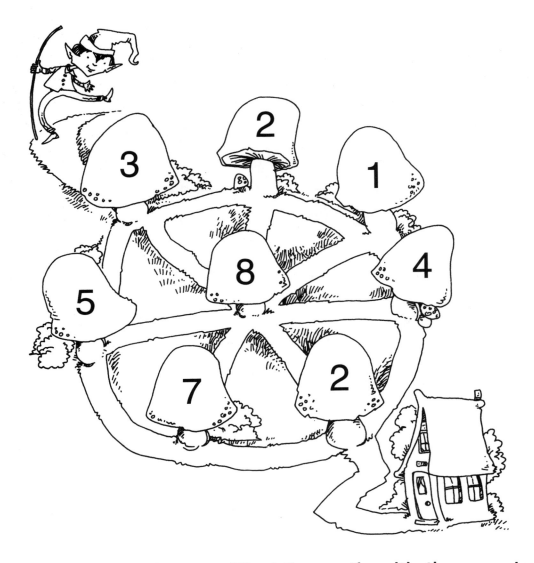

For an extra challenge: Find the path with the greatest sum. Draw the path with a different color.

Number Grid

Use the clues to fill in the boxes with the numbers 1 to 9.
Use each number only once.

A1: This number is the same as the number of days in a week.

A2: This number is even.

A3: This number is the smallest number in the grid.

B1: This number is half of A2.

B2: This number is one more than B1.

B3: This number is the sum of 7 + 2.

C1: This number is the sum of 3 + 3.

C2: This number is one less than C1.

C3: This number is one more than A1.

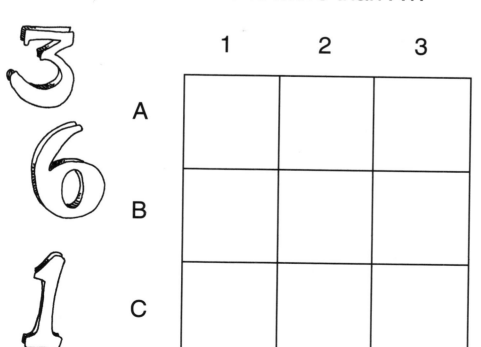

Subtraction Design

Solve the problems in the squares. Use a red crayon to color each square where the difference is 3. Color all the other squares green.

14 − 9	18 − 12	11 − 8	24 − 5	6 − 2
10 − 8	26 − 23	20 − 15	9 − 6	13 − 4
15 − 12	4 − 0	12 − 11	18 − 8	17 − 14
9 − 2	8 − 5	29 − 9	34 − 31	10 − 2
16 − 9	33 − 25	42 − 39	13 − 7	19 − 5

What pattern do the red squares make? _____

Gumball Math

Solve the problems on the gumballs.

If the answer on a gumball is 2, color it blue.

If the answer on a gumball is 3, color it red.

If the answer on a gumball is 4, color it green.

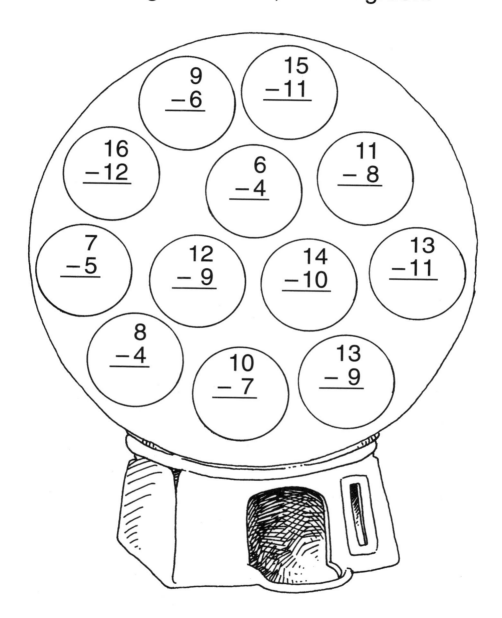

Noah bought 4 gumballs. Angie bought 3 gumballs.
How many gumballs were left in the machine? _____

Subtraction Design

Solve the problems in the squares. Use a blue crayon to color each square where the difference is 5. Color all the other squares yellow.

10 − 5	7 − 3	11 − 4	3 − 1	17 − 12
20 − 13	16 − 11	14 − 8	9 − 4	6 − 5
9 − 2	4 − 4	12 − 7	18 − 9	23 − 12
17 − 5	8 − 3	30 − 20	11 − 6	19 − 16
24 − 19	33 − 5	27 − 18	16 − 3	5 − 0

What pattern do the blue squares make? _____

Crazy Quilt

Color the squares of the quilt using only the colors red, yellow, green, and blue. Make sure that no squares of the same color touch—not even at the corners!

For an extra challenge: Can you figure out how many squares are on the quilt without counting them all? Solve this multiplication problem to find the answer:

3 squares in each row × 4 rows = _____ squares

Liam's Lunch

Liam has $1 to buy his lunch. What could he buy with his money? Below and on the next page, draw a circle around each tray that shows a combination of items that Liam could buy.

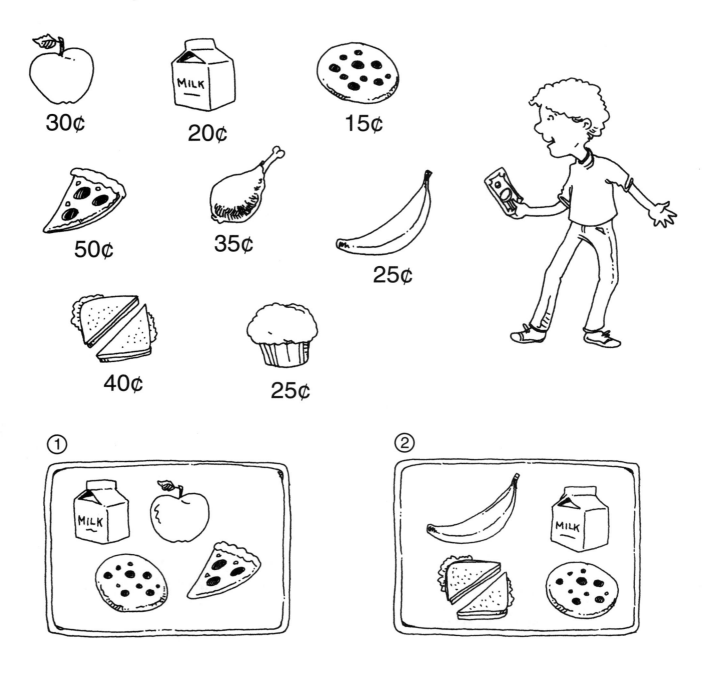

Find another combination of at least 3 items that Liam could buy with his money. Draw the items on the tray below.

How Many Spots?

Spike, Mike, and Ike are playful dalmatians. Use the clues below to figure out how many spots each dog has.

Spike has 20 more spots than Mike.

Mike has half as many spots as Ike.

Ike has as many spots as there are minutes in an hour.

Spike has _____ spots.

Mike has _____ spots.

Ike has _____ spots.

Up, Up, and Away!

Use the numbers on the cloud to fill in the missing numbers on the hot-air balloons. Use each number only once.

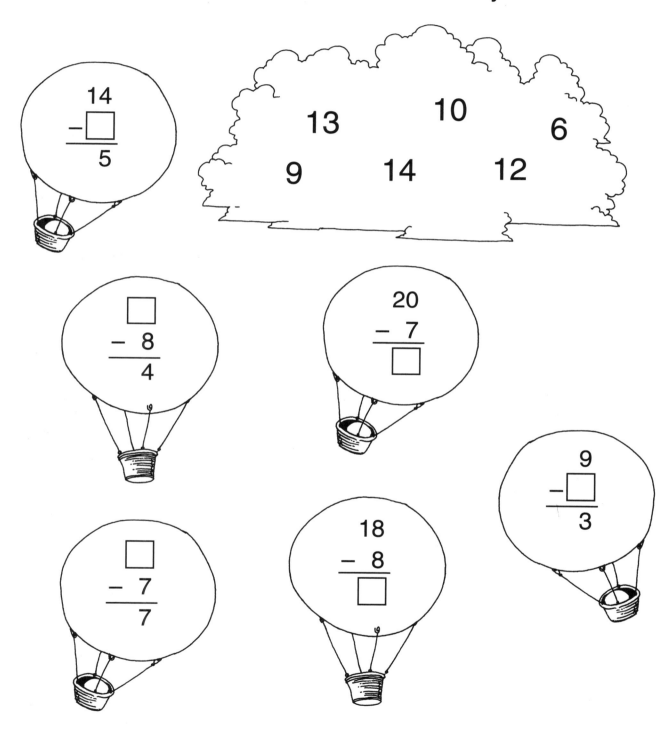

Penguin Parade

The penguins are supposed to be lined up according to their numbers, from smallest to largest. But some penguins are not in the right place!

In each row, circle the penguin that is out of order.

BIG Numbers

Numbers can be spelled out or written with a symbol—
one, two, three, or 1, 2, 3. The symbols for numbers are
called **numerals**.

Rewrite each number below using numerals.

1. Four hundred thirty-seven _____

2. Three thousand three _____

3. One thousand six hundred forty-one _____

4. Nine hundred seventy-six _____

5. Two thousand five hundred _____

Now write the numbers in numerals on the alligators in
order from smallest to largest.

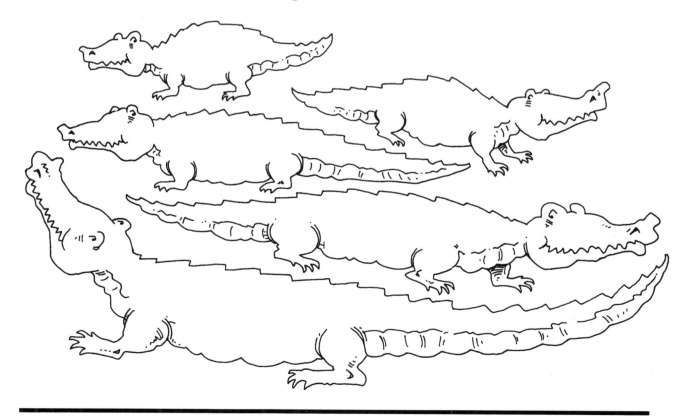

Tennis, Anyone?

The tennis partners are wearing sweaters with numbers that add up to 30.

Draw a line to connect each pair of partners.

Even Steven

Draw a line through each box so that the sum of the numbers on each side of the line is equal.

Hints: The line does not have to be straight.
There may be more than one solution.

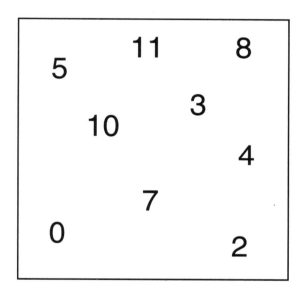

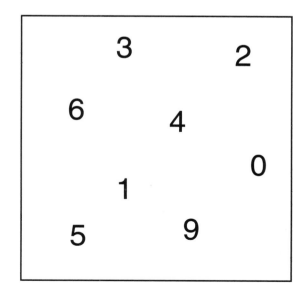

Coin Combinations

Draw 10 coins in any combination of nickels, dimes, and quarters to show at least three different ways to make $1.

Draw the coins like this:

			= $1

	= $1

	= $1

Piggy Banks

How much money is in each piggy bank? Add up the coins in each bank and write the total on the line below the bank.

1.

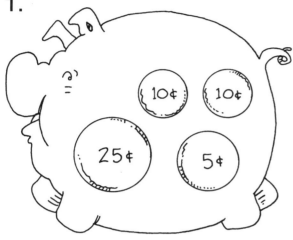

_____

2.

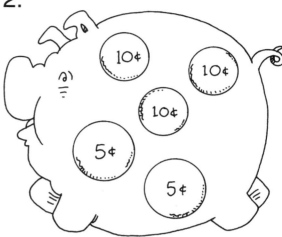

_____

3.

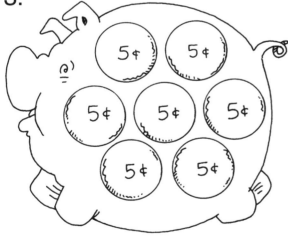

_____

4.

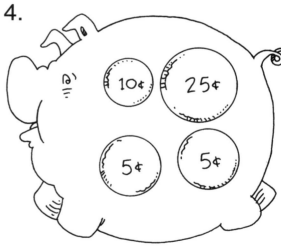

_____

Which piggy bank contains the most money? _____

Which piggy bank contains the least money? _____

Cat Math

Solve the addition or subtraction problem on each cat.
Some of the cats have the same answer. Color those cats
orange. Color the rest of the cats any way you like.

For an extra challenge: See if you can figure out the
answer to this problem: If 6 cats each had 2 kittens,
how many cats and kittens would there be altogether?

Bug Buddies

Draw 2 caterpillars on each of the 4 leaves.

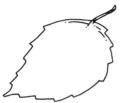  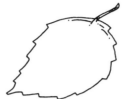 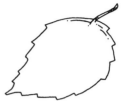

How many caterpillars are there altogether?

4 leaves × 2 caterpillars on each leaf = _____ caterpillars

Draw 5 bees on each of the 2 flowers.

How many bees are there altogether?

2 flowers × 5 bees on each flower = _____ bees

Draw 6 ants on each of the 3 sandwiches.

How many ants are there altogether?

3 sandwiches × 6 ants on each sandwich = _____ ants

Clown Math

These clowns love to juggle strange objects! Solve each of the multiplication problems on the objects they're juggling.

What is the answer on the object that is a fruit? _____

What is the answer on the object that is a musical instrument? _____

Home on the Range

Cowboy Sam is riding through Math Country. Help him on his journey by solving each of the multiplication problems.

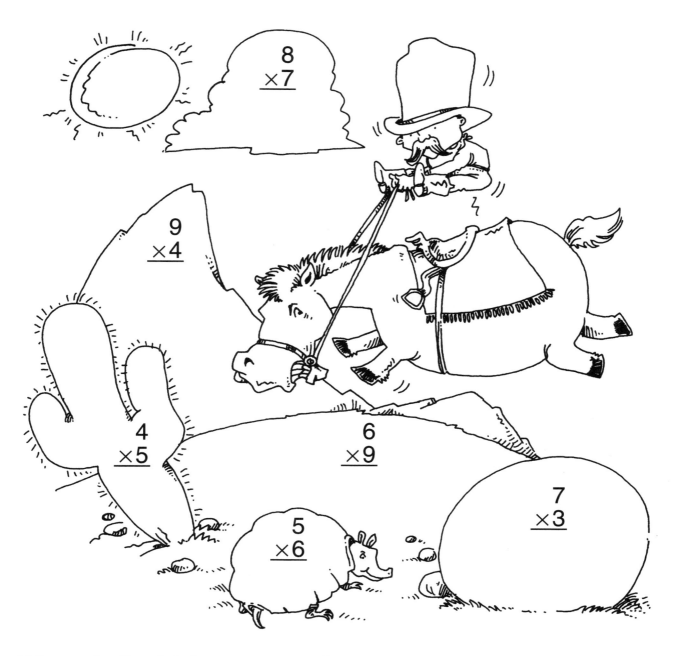

$$\begin{array}{r} 8 \\ \times 7 \\ \hline \end{array}$$

$$\begin{array}{r} 9 \\ \times 4 \\ \hline \end{array}$$

$$\begin{array}{r} 4 \\ \times 5 \\ \hline \end{array}$$

$$\begin{array}{r} 6 \\ \times 9 \\ \hline \end{array}$$

$$\begin{array}{r} 7 \\ \times 3 \\ \hline \end{array}$$

$$\begin{array}{r} 5 \\ \times 6 \\ \hline \end{array}$$

Where is the highest answer? _____

Where is the lowest answer? _____

Under the Sea

Miranda the Mermaid loves math! Solve each of the multiplication problems in her undersea home.

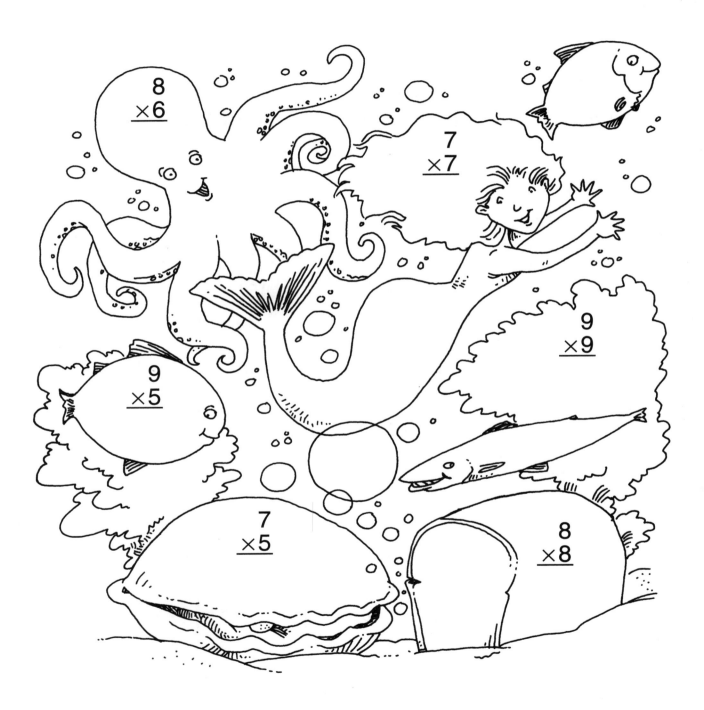

Super Snake

Even numbers are numbers that can be divided into two equal groups. **Odd numbers** are numbers that cannot be divided into two equal groups.

Complete each problem on the snake. Use a red crayon to color each section that contains an even answer. Use black to color each section that contains an odd answer.

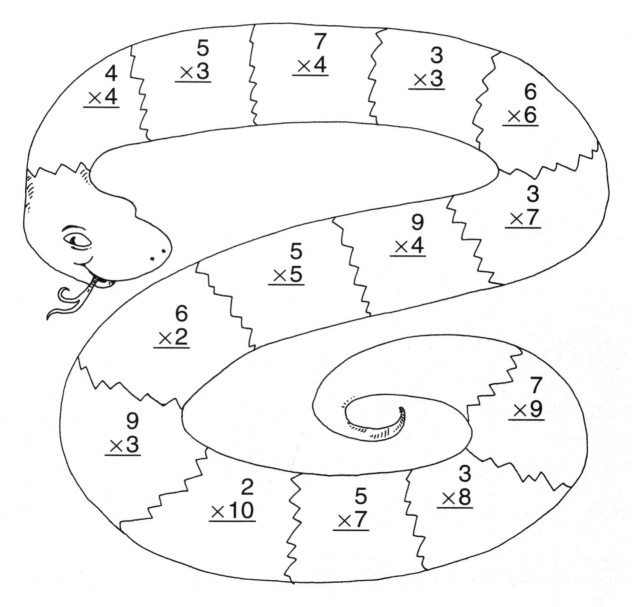

Fun at the Fair!

The town of Summerville just held its annual fair. Lots of people came to celebrate and have fun!

67 people rode the Ferris wheel on Saturday.
82 people rode it on Sunday.
How many people rode the Ferris wheel over the weekend? _____
How many more people rode it on Sunday than on Saturday? _____

The popcorn man bought a 25-pound bag of popcorn for the fair.
He popped 9 pounds on Saturday and 11 pounds on Sunday.
How many pounds of popcorn did he pop? _____
How many pounds of popcorn were left over? _____

Tricia played "Guess My Weight." The man at the booth thought Tricia weighed 73 pounds. She really weighs 6 pounds less. How much does Tricia weigh?

_____

99 hot dogs were sold on Saturday.

58 people put ketchup on their hot dogs.

The rest of the people put mustard on their hot dogs.

How many people put mustard on their hot dogs? _____

How many more people used ketchup than

mustard? _____

Patrick got in line to ride the roller coaster at 1:21 p.m.

The next ride was scheduled to begin at 2:00 p.m.

How many minutes did Patrick have to wait? _____

19 cherry pies, 15 blueberry pies, and 23 apple pies were

entered in the baking contest.

How many pies were entered altogether? _____

8 pies were awarded ribbons.

How many pies did not receive ribbons? _____

Number Stories

Use the numbers in the box above each story to fill in the missing numbers in a way that makes sense.

40	5	8

Mrs. Dickson runs _____ miles each day that she runs. She runs _____ days each week. Mrs. Dickson runs a total of _____ miles each week.

5	20	4

Suzanne's grandmother gave her _____ dollars for her birthday. The money was inside a birthday card. Inside the card there were _____ bills. Each bill was worth _____ dollars.

6	4	24

Anthony takes a spelling test every Friday. He takes about _____ tests each month. After _____ months, Anthony has taken about _____ spelling tests.

Creating Problems

You can create multiplication problems using objects you find around your house. Here are some examples:

How many cars does your family have? __2__
How many wheels are on each car? __4__
How many wheels are there in all?
    2 cars × 4 wheels on each car
    2 × 4 = 8 wheels

How many pairs of socks
are in your drawer? _____
How many socks are
there in each pair? __2__
How many socks do you have in all?
    _____ pairs × 2 socks in each pair
    _____ × 2 = _____ socks

Make up some more problems like these in the space below.

Let's Go Fishing!

The fish below and on the next page come in matching pairs. Each matching pair has the same answer.

Solve the problems on all the fish to discover the matching pairs. Color each matching pair a different color.

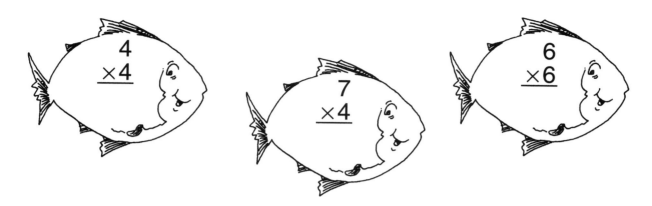

For an extra challenge: Create a drawing in the space below that shows this problem in pictures.

Problem: 3 boys went fishing. They each caught 6 fish. How many fish did they catch altogether?

At the Movies

Use the information in the story to answer the questions below.

A group of girl scouts went to see a movie. 12 girls bought root beer. 9 girls bought lemonade. 2 girls did not buy anything to drink. 4 girls sat in the front row. 6 girls sat in the back row. The rest of the girls sat in the middle of the theater. All the girls bought something to eat. 14 girls bought popcorn. 16 girls bought candy. The movie was 2 hours long and ended at 6:30 p.m.

1. How many girls went to the movie? _____
2. How many girls sat in the middle of the theater? _____
3. How many girls bought both popcorn and candy? _____
4. What time did the movie start? _____

A Pond Party

Use the information in the story to answer the questions below.

One lovely summer afternoon, some frogs had a party at Coolwater Pond. 15 frogs were green. 11 frogs were brown. 3 frogs were yellow. The biggest frog ate 5 mosquitoes and 6 flies. 10 frogs ate 3 mosquitoes each. 4 frogs ate 2 flies each. 14 frogs ate just 1 fly each. Each frog sat on a separate lily pad. There were 5 extra lily pads in the pond.

1. How many frogs came to the party? _____
2. How many bugs did the biggest frog eat? _____
3. How many mosquitoes were eaten altogether? _____
4. How many flies were eaten altogether? _____
5. How many lily pads were in the pond? _____

Special Number

Randy wants a special number for his basketball jersey. Read the clues to help him find it. Each clue will help you eliminate one or more numbers on the grid.

Place an **X** on each number that you eliminate.

This number has more than one digit.

Both digits in this number are greater than 2.

This number is odd.

The digit in the tens place is smaller than the digit in the ones place.

The sum of the digits is greater than 15.

The sum of the digits is an even number.

What is Randy's special number? _____

1	2	3	4	5	6	7	8	9	10
11	12	13	14	15	16	17	18	19	20
21	22	23	24	25	26	27	28	29	30
31	32	33	34	35	36	37	38	39	40
41	42	43	44	45	46	47	48	49	50
51	52	53	54	55	56	57	58	59	60
61	62	63	64	65	66	67	68	69	70
71	72	73	74	75	76	77	78	79	80
81	82	83	84	85	86	87	88	89	90
91	92	93	94	95	96	97	98	99	100

Measure for Measure

Fill in each blank space in the sentences below with a unit of measurement from the word box. Use each word only once.

inches	ounces	cups
feet	pounds	quarts
miles	tons	gallons

1. The recipe calls for 2 _____ of sugar.

2. We drove 250 _____ on our vacation.

3. The elephant weighed about 3 _____.

4. Dad put 12 _____ of gas in the car.

5. Judy's flower garden is 20 _____ long.

6. The baby drank 4 _____ of milk.

7. Nick's bowling ball weighs 12 _____.

8. The hummingbird was only 3 _____ long.

9. There are 4 _____ in a gallon.

Secret Number

What secret number does Megan have in
her magic hat? Read the clues to find out.
Each clue will help you eliminate one or
more numbers on the grid. Place an **X**
on each number that you eliminate.

The secret number has two digits.
The secret number is not odd.
The secret number does not contain a zero.
The first digit is not greater than the second digit.
The first digit is not smaller than the second digit.
The sum of the digits is greater than 5 but less than 10.

What is the secret number? _____

1	2	3	4	5	6	7	8	9	10
11	12	13	14	15	16	17	18	19	20
21	22	23	24	25	26	27	28	29	30
31	32	33	34	35	36	37	38	39	40
41	42	43	44	45	46	47	48	49	50
51	52	53	54	55	56	57	58	59	60
61	62	63	64	65	66	67	68	69	70
71	72	73	74	75	76	77	78	79	80
81	82	83	84	85	86	87	88	89	90
91	92	93	94	95	96	97	98	99	100

Such a Square

Divide each square into 4 equal parts. Make sure each square is divided differently from the others.

Half and Half

Draw a line through each figure below to divide the figure in half. Draw the line so that each half is the mirror image, or exact opposite, of the other.

Hint: For some of the figures, there is more than one way to divide the figure in half.

Fruit Fractions

Fill in each blank with the name of the fruit that makes the sentence true.

3/4 of the _____ have leaves.

3/6 of the _____ have leaves.

4/6 of the _____ have leaves.

5/6 of the _____ have leaves.

plums

apples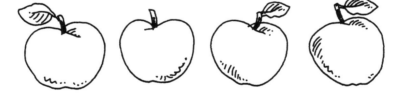

pears

peaches

Equivalent Fractions

Fractions that are written differently but mean the same amount are called **equivalent fractions**.

Color the shapes as directed to show some equivalent fractions.

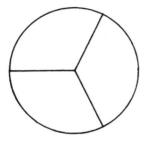

Color 2/3 of the circle.

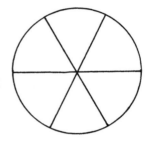

Color 4/6 of the circle.

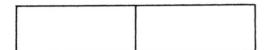

Color 1/2 of the rectangle.

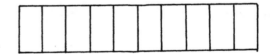

Color 5/10 of the rectangle.

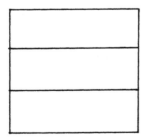

Color 1/3 of the square.

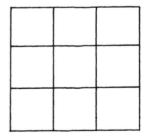

Color 3/9 of the square.

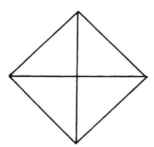

Color 1/4 of the diamond.

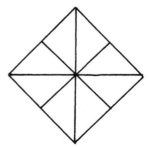

Color 2/8 of the diamond.

Matching Fractions

Draw a line to connect each fraction on the left to its equivalent fraction on the right. Match the equivalent fractions, and you will match each adult animal to its baby!

fox	2/16		4/10	kid
horse	1/2		2/3	pup
goat	2/5		1/8	kit
whale	1/3		6/12	foal
bear	1/4		2/6	calf
seal	6/9		2/8	cub

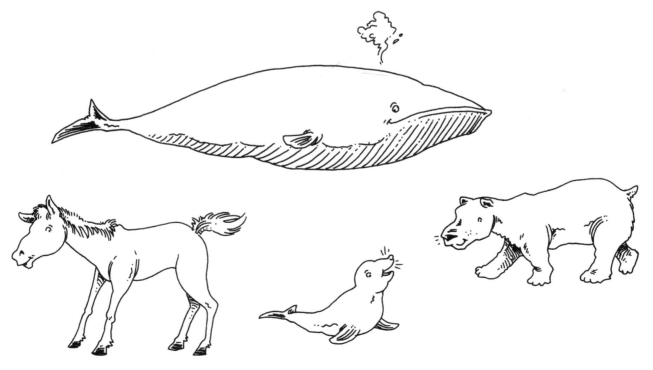

Candy Counter

Color some lollipops red and some yellow. Make sure there are the same number of red and yellow lollipops.

Color some jelly beans black, some green, and some orange. Make sure there are the same number of each color.

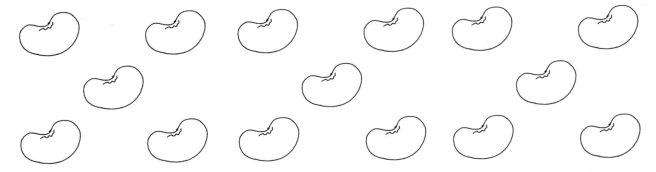

Color some jelly bears purple, some red, some green, and some yellow. Make sure there are the same number of each color.

Color some jaw breakers pink, some blue, and some yellow. Make sure there are the same number of each color.

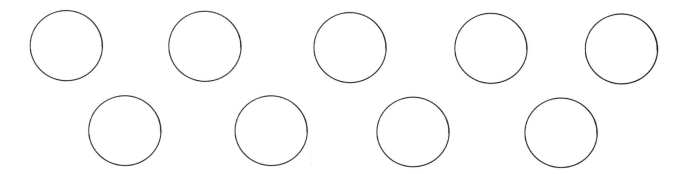

Color some candy canes red and some green. Make sure there are the same number of each color.

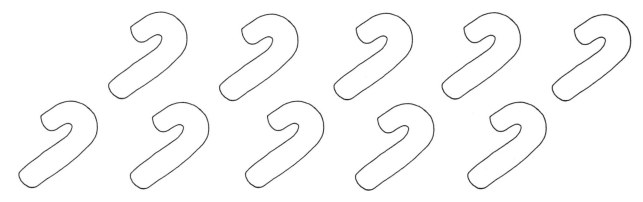

Color some pieces of taffy purple, some brown, some orange, and some green. Make sure there are the same number of each color.

The Sun City Softball Team

Look at the graph below. It shows how many runs each player on the Sun City softball team scored for the season.

	1	2	3	4	5	6	7	8	9	10
Carol	▨	▨	▨							
Joe	▨	▨	▨	▨	▨	▨	▨	▨	▨	▨
Tom	▨	▨	▨	▨	▨	▨				
Cindy	▨	▨	▨	▨	▨	▨	▨			
Jean	▨	▨								
Ted	▨	▨	▨							
Rex	▨									
Ross	▨	▨	▨	▨	▨	▨	▨			
Lisa	▨	▨	▨	▨	▨					

Use the information on the graph to answer these questions.

1. Who scored the most runs? _____
2. How many runs did Ross and Cindy score altogether? _____
3. Did Lisa score more runs than Tom? _____
4. Which two players scored the same number of runs?

_____

A Pair of Flippers

The scuba diver has a trunk full of flippers. Half the flippers in the trunk are black. The other half are white.

If the diver shuts his eyes and takes out one flipper at a time, how many flippers does he have to pull out before he can be sure that he has a matching pair?

Answer: _____

Mission to Mars

Ned, Nelly, and Nikki are astronauts on a mission to Mars.

Solve each of the problems below and on the next page. Write addition, subtraction, or multiplication problems to show how you got your answers.

1. Each astronaut has 8 zippers on his or her space suit. How many zippers are there altogether?

2. Ned has found 9 new stars in space. Nikki has found twice as many stars as Ned. How many stars have Ned and Nikki found altogether?

3. Each astronaut has been on 12 missions to outer space. How many missions have they been on altogether?

4. The astronauts brought 75 packages of space ice cream with them. In the first week, each astronaut ate 6 packages. How many packages of space ice cream were left at the end of the first week?

5. The trip to Mars will take 37 days. The astronauts left Earth 9 days ago. How many more days will it take for the astronauts to arrive at Mars?

6. Nelly did a space walk for 38 minutes. She started the space walk at 10:07. What time did the space walk end?

Where's Wally?

Wally was the only boy to get a perfect score on the second grade math test.

Use the clues to find out which boy is Wally. In each pair of statements, one statement is true and the other is false. Draw a circle around Wally.

Wally has freckles. Wally has a bow tie.
Wally has big ears. Wally has a missing tooth.
Wally has straight hair. Wally has small ears.
Wally has curly hair. Wally has big ears.
Wally has a missing tooth. Wally has a bow tie.

Favorite Lakes

Rena, Dena, and Lena like to go canoeing on beautiful lakes. Use the clues below to find out each girl's age and the name of her favorite lake.

The girl who is oldest likes Jenny Lake.

The oldest girl is 2 years older than the youngest girl.

The girl who is 13 likes Loon Lake.

Rena likes String Lake.

The youngest girl is 12.

Dena is not the oldest girl.

Name	Age	Favorite Lake

Camping Out

Mack, Jack, and Zack went camping. Use the clues below to find out the color of each boy's tent and what kind of food each boy brought along.

The boy who brought cookies has a green tent.

Jack does not have a green tent.

Zack did not bring hot dogs.

Mack has a red tent.

The boy who brought chili has a blue tent.

Name	Tent	Food

Answers

Page 5

1   3   5   7   9
11   13   15   17

If there were one more problem, the answer would be 19.

10	7	15	1
8	11	4	9
12	19	3	17
20	16	14	13
6	2	18	5

The colored squares make the number 9.

Page 6

6   7   8   9
10   11   12   13

Any two addition problems whose answers are 14 and 15 would continue the pattern.

14	8	11
3	16	6
5	15	13
17	4	9
7	10	12

The colored squares make the number 3.

Page 7

W   P   A   S   O   I
9   12   15   14   16   19

T   B   L   V   Y   E
13   18   17   10   8   21

ALWAYS "BEE" POSITIVE

Page 8

$1 + \mathbf{1} = 2 + \mathbf{3} = 5 + 3 = \mathbf{8}$
$4 + \mathbf{1} = \mathbf{5} + 2 = 7 + \mathbf{2} = 9$
$2 + 2 = \mathbf{4} + \mathbf{3} = 7 + \mathbf{3} = 10$
$\mathbf{3} + 3 = \mathbf{6} + 2 = 8 + \mathbf{4} = 12$
$\mathbf{6} + 4 = \mathbf{10} + 3 = \mathbf{13} + 2 = 15$
$6 + \mathbf{6} = \mathbf{12} + 2 = 14 + \mathbf{4} = 18$

Page 9

Pages 10–11

PIG
P = 16   I = 9   G = 7
16 + 9 + 7 = **32**
BOX
B = 2   O = 15   X = 24
2 + 15 + 24 = **41**
MAN
M = 13   A = 1   N = 14
13 + 1 + 14 = **28**
FARM
F = 6   A = 1   R = 18   M = 13
6 + 1 + 18 + 13 = **38**
KING
K = 11   I = 9   N = 14   G = 7
11 + 9 + 14 + 7 = **41**
HAND
H = 8   A = 1   N = 14   D = 4
8 + 1 + 14 + 4 = **27**
ROSE
R = 18   O = 15   S = 19   E = 5
18 + 15 + 19 + 5 = **57**

ROSE has the highest value. HAND has the lowest value.
Extra challenge: Answers will vary.

Page 12

Page 13

Page 14

Path with lowest sum:

Path with highest sum:

Page 15

	1	2	3
A	7	4	1
B	2	3	9
C	6	5	8

Page 16

14 −9 = 5	18 −12 = 6	11 −8 = 3	24 −5 = 19	6 −2 = 4
10 −8 = 2	26 −23 = 3	20 −15 = 5	9 −6 = 3	13 −4 = 9
15 −12 = 3	4 −0 = 4	12 −11 = 1	18 −8 = 10	17 −14 = 3
9 −2 = 7	8 −5 = 3	29 −9 = 20	34 −31 = 3	10 −2 = 8
16 −9 = 7	33 −25 = 8	42 −39 = 3	13 −7 = 6	19 −5 = 14

G	G	R	G	G
G	R	G	R	G
R	G	G	G	R
G	R	G	R	G
G	G	R	G	G

The red squares create a diamond pattern.

Page 17

9 − 6 = 3   red
15 − 11 = 4   green
16 − 12 = 4   green
6 − 4 = 2   blue
11 − 8 = 3   red
7 − 5 = 2   blue
12 − 9 = 3   red
14 − 10 = 4   green
13 − 11 = 2   blue
8 − 4 = 4   green
10 − 7 = 3   red
13 − 9 = 4   green

5 gumballs were left in the machine.

Page 18

10 − 5 = 5	7 − 3 = 4	11 − 4 = 7	3 − 1 = 2	17 − 12 = 5
20 − 13 = 7	16 − 11 = 5	14 − 8 = 6	9 − 4 = 5	6 − 5 = 1
9 − 2 = 7	4 − 4 = 0	12 − 7 = 5	18 − 9 = 9	23 − 12 = 11
17 − 5 = 12	8 − 3 = 5	30 − 20 = 10	11 − 6 = 5	19 − 16 = 3
24 − 19 = 5	33 − 5 = 28	27 − 18 = 9	16 − 3 = 13	5 − 0 = 5

B	Y	Y	Y	B
Y	B	Y	B	Y
Y	Y	B	Y	Y
Y	B	Y	B	Y
B	Y	Y	Y	B

The blue squares create an X.

Page 19

There are several solutions. This is one possible pattern:

R	Y	R
B	G	B
R	Y	R
B	G	B

Extra challenge: 12 squares

Pages 20–21

Tray 1: $1.15   Tray 2: $1
Tray 3: $1.10   Tray 4: $1
Tray 5: $0.95   Tray 6: $1.10
Circle trays 2, 4, and 5.
Parent: Make sure child draws 3 or 4 food items on empty tray whose total cost is $1 or less.

Page 22

Spike has 50 spots.
Mike has 30 spots.
Ike has 60 spots.

Page 23

14 − **9** = 5   **14** − 7 = 7
12 − 8 = 4   18 − 8 = **10**
20 − 7 = **13**   9 − **6** = 3

Page 24

The penguins with these numbers should be circled:

Row 1: 39   Row 3: 29
Row 2: 83   Row 4: 42

Page 25

1. 437   4. 976
2. 3003   5. 2500
3. 1641

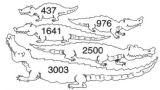

Page 26

Tennis players should be matched up like this:
16—14
11—19
20—10
18—12

Page 27

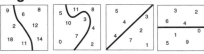

Page 28

2 quarters, 2 dimes, 6 nickels
10 dimes
1 quarter, 6 dimes, 3 nickels

Page 29

Bank 1: 50¢   Bank 2: 40¢
Bank 3: 35¢   Bank 4: 45¢
Bank 1 contains the most money.
Bank 3 contains the least money.

Page 30

60 + 20 = 80
42 − 30 = 12
50 − 28 = 22
36 + 34 = 70 orange
48 + 22 = 70 orange
34 − 17 = 17
54 + 16 = 70 orange
47 − 29 = 18

Extra challenge:

2 + 2 + 2 + 2 + 2 + 2 = 12 kittens *or*
6 cats × 2 kittens each = 12 kittens
6 cats + 12 kittens = 18 cats and kittens altogether

Page 31

8 caterpillars
10 bees
18 ants

Page 32

4 × 6 = 24   3 × 5 = 15
5 × 4 = 20   6 × 3 = 18
2 × 5 = 10   8 × 2 = 16
7 × 4 = 28   9 × 3 = 27
The answer on the pineapple is 20.
The answer on the tambourine is 24.

Page 33

8 × 7 = 56   6 × 9 = 54
9 × 4 = 36   5 × 6 = 30
4 × 5 = 20   7 × 3 = 21
The highest answer is on the cloud.
The lowest answer is on the cactus.

Page 34

8 × 6 = 48   9 × 9 = 81
7 × 7 = 49   7 × 5 = 35
9 × 5 = 45   8 × 8 = 64

Page 35

4 × 4 = 16   5 × 5 = 25
5 × 3 = 15   6 × 2 = 12
7 × 4 = 28   9 × 3 = 27
3 × 3 = 9   2 × 10 = 20
6 × 6 = 36   5 × 7 = 35
3 × 7 = 21   3 × 8 = 24
9 × 4 = 36   7 × 9 = 63

Pages 36–37

149 people rode the Ferris wheel over the weekend.
15 more people rode it on Sunday than on Saturday.
He popped 20 pounds of popcorn.
5 pounds of popcorn were left over.
Tricia weighs 67 pounds.
41 people put mustard on their hot dogs.
17 more people used ketchup than mustard.
Patrick had to wait 39 minutes.
57 pies were entered altogether.
49 pies did not receive ribbons.

Page 38

8 miles each day
5 days each week

40 miles each week
20 dollars
4 bills
5 dollars
4 tests each month
6 months
24 spelling tests

Page 39
Problems will vary.

Pages 40–41
The matching pairs of fish have these problems and answers:
$6 \times 2 = 12$ and $3 \times 4 = 12$
$8 \times 3 = 24$ and $6 \times 4 = 24$
$4 \times 5 = 20$ and $10 \times 2 = 20$
$9 \times 4 = 36$ and $6 \times 6 = 36$
$14 \times 2 = 28$ and $7 \times 4 = 28$
$2 \times 8 = 16$ and $4 \times 4 = 16$
Parent: Make sure child colors each pair of fish a different color.
Extra challenge: *Parent:* Child could draw 3 boys each holding 6 fish, or 3 groups of 6 fish to show 18 fish altogether.

Page 42
1. $12 + 9 + 2 = 23$ girls
2. $23 - 4 = 19$; $19 - 6 = 13$
   13 girls sat in the middle of the theater.
3. $14 + 16 = 30$; $30 - 23 = 7$
   7 girls bought both popcorn and candy.
4. 4:30 p.m.

Page 43
1. $15 + 11 + 3 = 29$ frogs
2. $5 + 6 = 11$ bugs
3. $10 \times 3 = 30$; $5 + 30 = 35$ mosquitoes
4. $4 \times 2 = 8$; $6 + 8 + 14 = 28$ flies
5. $29 + 5 = 34$ lily pads

Page 44
Randy's special number is 79.

Page 45
1. cups
2. miles
3. tons
4. gallons
5. feet
6. ounces
7. pounds
8. inches
9. quarts

Page 46
The secret number is 44.

Page 47
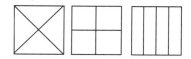

Page 48
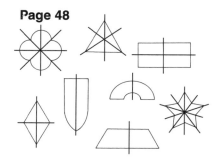

Page 49
3/4 of the apples have leaves.
3/6 of the pears have leaves.
4/6 of the peaches have leaves.
5/6 of the plums have leaves.

Page 50
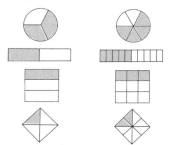

Page 51
Animals and fractions should be matched up like this:
fox 2/16—1/8 kit
horse 1/2—6/12 foal
goat 2/5—4/10 kid
whale 1/3—2/6 calf
bear 1/4—2/8 cub
seal 6/9—2/3 pup

Pages 52–53
Parent: Make sure child colors the candy items as follows:
Lollipops: 4 red, 4 yellow
Jelly beans: 5 black, 5 green, 5 orange
Jelly bears: 3 purple, 3 red, 3 green, 3 yellow
Jaw breakers: 3 pink, 3 blue, 3 yellow
Candy canes: 5 red, 5 green
Taffy: 4 purple, 4 brown, 4 orange, 4 green

Page 54
1. Joe. He scored 10 runs.
2. 15. Ross scored 8 runs and Cindy scored 7.
3. No. Lisa scored 5 runs and Tom scored 6.
4. Carol and Ted. Both scored 3 runs.

Page 55
3 flippers
The first flipper he pulls out could be white or black.
The second flipper he pulls out could be white or black.
He could have a matching pair after pulling out 2 flippers, or he could have 2 different flippers.
To be sure he has a matching pair, he must pull out a third flipper. The third flipper will match either the first or second flipper, since there are only two colors.

Pages 56–57
1. $8 + 8 + 8 = 24$ *or*
   $3 \times 8 = 24$ zippers
2. Stars Nikki found: $2 \times 9 = 18$
   $9 + 18 = 27$ stars
3. $12 + 12 + 12 = 36$ *or*
   $3 \times 12 = 36$ missions
4. Ice cream eaten in the first week:
   $6 + 6 + 6 = 18$ *or*
   $3 \times 6 = 18$ packages eaten
   $75 - 18 = 57$ packages left
5. $37 - 9 = 28$ more days
6. $38 + 7 = 45$
   The space walk ended at 10:45.

Page 58
Wally is the middle boy in the top row.

Page 59
Name	Age	Favorite Lake
Rena	12	String Lake
Dena	13	Loon Lake
Lena	14	Jenny Lake

Page 60
Name	Tent	Food
Mack	red	hot dogs
Jack	blue	chili
Zack	green	cookies

Other

books that will help develop your child's gifts and talents

Workbooks:
- Reading (4–6) $4.95
- Reading Book Two (4–6) $4.95
- Math (4–6) $4.95
- Math Book Two (4–6) $4.95
- Language Arts (4–6) $4.95
- Puzzles & Games for
  Reading and Math (4–6) $4.95
- Puzzles & Games for
  Reading and Math Book Two (4–6) $4.95
- Puzzles & Games for
  Critical and Creative Thinking (4–6) $4.95
- Phonics (4–6) $4.95
- Phonics Puzzles & Games (4–6) $4.95
- Math Puzzles & Games (4–6) $4.95
- Reading Puzzles & Games (4–6) $4.95
- Reading (6–8) $4.95
- Reading Book Two (6–8) $4.95
- Math (6–8) $4.95
- Math Book Two (6–8) $4.95
- Language Arts (6–8) $4.95
- Puzzles & Games for
  Reading and Math (6–8) $4.95
- Puzzles & Games for
  Reading and Math, Book Two (6–8) $4.95
- Puzzles & Games for
  Critical and Creative Thinking (6–8) $4.95
- Phonics (6–8) $4.95
- Phonics Puzzles & Games (6–8) $4.95
- Math Puzzles & Games (6–8) $4.95
- Reading Puzzles & Games (6–8) $4.95
- Reading Comprehension (6–8) $4.95

Reference Workbooks:
- Word Book (4–6) $4.95
- Almanac (6–8) $3.95
- Atlas (6–8) $3.95
- Dictionary (6–8) $3.95

Story Starters:
- My First Stories (6–8) $5.95
- Stories About Me (6–8) $5.95
- Stories About Animals (6–8) $4.95

Science Workbooks:
- The Human Body (4–6) $5.95
- Animals (4–6) $5.95
- The Earth (4–6) $5.95
- The Ocean (4–6) $5.95

Question & Answer Books:
- The Gifted & Talented® Question &
  Answer Book for Ages 4–6 $5.95
- Gifted & Talented® More Questions &
  Answers for Ages 4–6 $5.95
- Gifted & Talented® Still More
  Questions & Answers for
  Ages 4–6 $5.95
- The Gifted & Talented® Question &
  Answer Book for Ages 6–8 $5.95
- Gifted & Talented® More Questions &
  Answers for Ages 6–8 $5.95
- Gifted & Talented® Still More
  Questions & Answers for
  Ages 6–8 $5.95
- Gifted & Talented® Science Questions
  & Answers: The Human Body
  for Ages 6–8 $5.95

For Preschoolers:
- Alphabet Workbook $5.95
- Counting Workbook $5.95

Drawing:
- Learn to Draw (6 and up) $5.95

For Parents:
- How to Develop Your Child's Gifts
  and Talents During the Elementary
  Years $11.95
- How to Develop Your Child's Gifts and
  Talents in Math $15.00
- How to Develop Your Child's Gifts and
  Talents in Reading $15.00
- How to Develop Your Child's Gifts and
  Talents in Vocabulary $15.00
- How to Develop Your Child's Gifts and
  Talents in Writing $15.00

For orders, call 1-800-323-4900.